From the Country
of Nevermore

To Merlin /
for all the help ... in 1978
" way back when —
right up to now !
Warmest regards
Mary

From the Country
of Nevermore

Selected Poems of Jorge Teillier

Translated and with an Introduction by Mary Crow

NE *Wesleyan University Press*

Published by University Press of New England

Hanover and London

The University Press of New England

is a consortium of universities in New England dedicated to publishing scholarly and trade works by authors from member campuses and elsewhere. The New England imprint signifies uniform standards for publication excellence maintained without exception by the consortium members. A joint imprint of University Press of New England and a sponsoring member acknowledges the publishing mission of that university and its support for the dissemination of scholarship throughout the world. Cited by the American Council of Learned Societies as a model to be followed, University Press of New England publishes books under its own imprint and the imprints of Brandeis University, Brown University, Clark University, University of Connecticut, Dartmouth College, University of New Hampshire, University of Rhode Island, Tufts University, University of Vermont, and Wesleyan University.

Most of the poems in *From the Country of Nevermore* were translated from *Muertes y maravillas,* © 1971, by permission of Editorial Universitaria. "Not a Sign of Life" and "Story about a Branch of Myrtle" were translated from *Cartas de reinas de otras primaveras,* © 1985 by Jorge Teillier.

Some of these translations appeared in these magazines: *The American Poetry Review, The Black Warrior Review, George Washington Review, Ground Water Review, International Poetry Review, Mississippi Valley Review, New Letters, New Mexico Humanities Review, Nimrod, The Poetry Miscellany, Southern Humanities Review, Willow Springs, Wooster Review,* and *Xavier Review.*

Library of Congress Cataloging-in-Publication Data

Teillier, Jorge.
From the country of Nevermore : poems / by Jorge Teillier : translated by Mary Crow. — 1st ed.
p. cm.
Translated from Spanish.
ISBN 0–8195–2176–0 — ISBN 0–8195–1178–1 (pbk.)
1. Teillier, Jorge—Translations, English. I. Crow, Mary.
II. Title.
PQ8098.3.E4A17   1990
861—dc20   89–28425
                                                 CIP

Printed in the United States of America

5   4   3   2   1

Wesleyan Poetry in Translation

Contents

III. The Land of Night

IV. I Would Give All the Gold in the World

Introduction

Jorge Teillier, who has been called the most important Chilean poet of his generation, was born in 1935 in Lautaro, in the south of Chile. Author of twelve collections of poems, he has also written short stories and essays, and edited literary magazines. But even though his poetry has been the subject of many articles, including a number in the United States, and Hispanic scholars have been discussing it for some years, his work has not been available to the general reader of poetry in English because of the lack of translation.

Teillier has a contemporary voice, influenced by the French Symbolists, by Edgar Allan Poe, and by his nostalgia for North American memorabilia of the twenties and thirties—old songs like "Paper Moon" and old-fashioned singers like Al Jolson. Typically, a Teillier poem is inhabited by Chile's southern countryside and its persistent rainy days, by the beliefs and superstitions of country people, by the sad sound of passing night trains on their way, perhaps, to happiness, and by death in its many incarnations. Yet, in spite of such imagery, Teillier's poems stop short of sentimentality through his use of simple matter-of-fact conclusions and by the exclusion of self-pity. If self-pity creeps in, it is accompanied by a saving self-mockery.

There is no other voice in contemporary poetry quite like Teillier's, which has been accorded a recognition in Chile and Latin America that it deserves to receive in other countries. His reputation has begun to spread around the world, and some of his poems are being translated into French, Italian, Swedish, Czechoslovakian, Russian, Rumanian, and Polish, as well as English. The translations of his work into English have, until now, appeared only in literary magazines, in translations by Miller Williams, Margaret Sayers Peden, John Upton, and Carolyn Wright; in *Anthology of Magazine Verse and Yearbook of American Poetry*, 1987; and in a broadsheet.

Jorge Teillier began writing poems when he was twelve. At that time he loved to read fiction, especially Jules Verne and other "fairy tales," and such books influenced his poetry. One of his earliest and most persistent favorites among poets was Edgar Allan Poe; Teillier's mature work retains more than a trace of Poe's nostalgia and mystery. His first book, *Para angeles y gorriones* (For Angels and Sparrows), appeared when he was twenty-one. By then he was interested in the work of Paul Verlaine, Rubén Darío, Vicente Huidobro, Teófilo Cid. As he read, he says, he began to wonder: What does *Chilean* mean? "Poetry," he concluded, "is universality. . . . The death before us is the death of the lutist of ancient Egypt, is also the death of Rilke, death is great and we belong to death, and the same snow is remembered in Villon and is like the solitude in Rilke, and time is a river in Heraclitus and Jorge Manrique." So, he says, he took the train back from Santiago, back to the provinces, to the rain and snow, the silence, solitude, and deserted stations of Chile's lovely South, full of snow-capped volcanoes, rivers, and lakes, small villages with plazas and patios. In those years of his development, his hero was Pablo Neruda, who lamented that young men were reading his Surrealist and literary *Residencia en la tierra* (Residence on Earth) instead of the simple words of his social-protest poems. Teillier, however, did not find that writing political poems came naturally to him, in spite of his sympathy with Neruda's complaint. His poems focus, instead, on the politics of the psyche or on poor, lovely, but ill-fated dreams of happiness.

Although Jorge Teillier studied history education at the University of Chile, he taught only one year. He then joined the editorial staff of the university's *Bulletin,* and eventually became its editor.

Among his books of poetry are *Para angeles y gorriones, El cielo cae con las hojas, El árbol de la memoria, Poemas del país de nunca jamás, Los trenes de la noche y otros poemas, Poemas secretos, Crónica del forastero, Muertes y maravillas, Para un pueblo fantasma,* and *Cartas para reinas de otras primaveras.* He has also published two collections of essays: *Romeo Murga, poeta adolescente* and *Actualidad de Vicinte*

Huidobro. In addition to his extensive writing for newspapers and literary magazines, he has translated poems from French into Spanish, and his poetry has appeared in magazines and anthologies throughout Latin America.

In 1986, in the introduction to *Cartas para reinas de otras primaveras,* fiction writer Jorge Edwards said, "In Teillier's poetry a mythical South exists, the same rainy and forested frontier of Pablo Neruda, but in this case made unreal, changed into a pretext for a verbal creation where trees, mountains, provincial plazas, are colored by innumerable references to contemporary literature, as if literary and natural space were interwoven. The phantasmagorical House of Usher, that in the story of Poe was brought down on top of his dream, floats in the verses of Teillier in a ghostly South, and the poet William Gray is cured of his delirium tremens in a clinic on the outskirts of Santiago."

Even now, Teillier lives in a timeless place of literature, dividing his days between a house in Santiago and a nearby country estate with an old wooden mill.

A Note on the Translation

It has been a pleasure to help introduce the poems of Jorge Teillier to English-language readers and to give Teillier the chance to join the "congregation of voices" of world literature. I used two premises. First, each translation into English must be a poem. To be a poem, the translation needs to achieve natural English that moves rhythmically. Second, each translation must keep as close as possible to the original, respecting the author's style, punctuation, lines—in short, everything—unless this results in awkward phrasing or syntax in English where there was no awkward phrasing or syntax in Spanish.

If the first is not achieved, there would be little reason to read the translations; after all, a book of translations is a book for readers of English. Given this constraint, I have tried to stay as close to my understanding of the author's intent as I could, while reproducing line and phrasing as far as possible. Of course, some effects are inevitably lost—alliteration, assonance and consonance, double meanings, and the range of connotations embedded in the phrasings Teillier uses. Other effects are gained.

Luckily for me, Teillier writes poetry that is highly translatable into English. This is partly because his poems are so image-laden and partly because the Poesque atmosphere will be familiar to readers of English.

In a few instances, a translation includes something not in the original. These are Teillier's changes; he asked me to include, for example, the words "in memoriam" in a dedication to a person who died after the poem's original publication. There are also a few old-fashioned English usages. These reflect allusions to a literary work translated into English, as in the case of "the snows of yesteryear" from François Villon, and quotations from an earlier period, such as the now archaic "nevermore" from Poe's "The Raven."

Most of the poems in this collection are from *Muertes y maravillas*

(Editorial Universitaria, 1971), a volume that collects a large body of Teillier's poetry. In my opinion, that is the strongest of his books. I have also chosen a few poems from his most recent book, *Cartas para reinas de otras primaveras* (Ediciones Manieristas, 1985), to demonstrate the range and variety of his writing.

I would like to express my gratitude for a Fulbright research grant, which took me to Chile in 1982 and led me to the poetry of Jorge Teillier. I would also like to thank Colorado State University, for a grant that allowed me to return in 1986, and Patsy Boyer, for her generous help and support in the revision of these translations.

I
Letter of Rain

Nieve nocturna

¿Es que puede existir algo antes de la nieve?
Antes de esa pureza implacable,
implacable como el mensaje de un mundo que no amamos
pero al cual pertenecemos
y que se adivina en ese sonido
todavia hermano del silencio.
¿Qué dedos te dejan caer,
pulverizado esqueleto de pétalos?
Ceniza de un cielo antiguo
que hace quedar solo frente al fuego
escuchando los pasos del amigo que se va,
eco de palabras que no recordamos,
pero que nos duelen como si las fuéramos a decir de nuevo.

¿Y puede existir algo después de la nieve,
algo después de la última mirada del ciego a la palidez del sol,
algo después que el niño enfermo olvida mirar la nueva mañana,
o, mejor aún, despúes de haber dormido como un convaleciente
con la cabeza sobre la falda
de aquella a quien alguna vez se ama?
¿Quién eres, nieve nocturna,
fugaz, disuelta primavera que sobrevive en el cerezo?
¿O qué importa quién eres?
Para mirar la nieve en la noche hay que cerrar los ojos,
no recordar nada, no preguntar nada.
desaparecer, deslizarse como ella en el visible silencio.

Night Snow

Can something exist before snow?
Before this implacable purity,
implacable as the message of a world
we don't love but belong to
and which can be divined in that sound,
still a brother of silence.
What fingers drop you,
pulverized skeleton of petals?
Ash of an ancient sky
that makes one remain alone before the fire
listening to the steps of the friend who leaves,
echo of words we don't remember, but that hurt us
as if we were going to say them once more.

And can something exist after snow?
Something after the last glance of the blind man at the sun's pallor,
something after the sick child forgets to look for the new morning,
or, more exactly, after a sleep like the sleep of a convalescent
with his head in the lap
of the woman he once loved?
Who are you, night snow?
Fleeting, dissolved spring that survives in the cherry tree?
Or does it matter who you are?
To look at the snow in the night one has to shut his eyes,
remember nothing, ask nothing,
disappear, slip away like snow into the visible silence.

Otoño secreto

Cuando las amadas palabras cotidianas
pierden su sentido
y no se puede nombrar ni el pan,
ni el agua, ni la ventana,
y ha sido falso todo diálogo que no sea
con nuestra desolada imagen,
aún se miran las destrozadas estampas
en el libro del hermano menor,
es bueno saludar los platos y el mantel puestos sobre la mesa,
y ver que en el viejo armario conservan su alegría
el licor de guindas que preparó la abuela
y las manzanas puestas a guardar.

Cuando la forma de los árboles
ya no es sino el leve recuerdo de su forma,
una mentira inventada
por la turbia memoria del otoño,
y los días tienen la confusión
del desván a donde nadie sube
y la cruel blancura de la eternidad
hace que la luz huya de sí misma,
algo nos recuerda la verdad
que amamos antes de conocer:
las ramas se quiebran levemente,
el palomar se llena de aleteos,
el granero sueña otra vez con el sol,
encendemos para la fiesta
los pálidos candelabros del salón polvoriento
y el silencio nos revela el secreto
que no queríamos escuchar.

Secret Autumn

When the loved daily words
lose their meaning
and bread cannot be named,
or water, or window,
and all dialogue has proven false
that wasn't with our own desolate image,
when you can still look over the tattered pictures
in your kid brother's book—
then it's good to greet the cloth and the dishes arranged on the table,
good to see that the cherry liqueur grandmother made
and the apples put by for safekeeping
conserve their happiness in the old sideboard.

When the form of trees
is merely the slight memory of their form,
a lie invented
by autumn's turbid memory,
and days have the confusion of the attic
no one climbs up to,
and the cruel whiteness of eternity
makes light flee from itself—
then something reminds us of the truth
we love even before we know it:
branches snap lightly,
the pigeon coop is filled with fluttering,
the granary dreams again of the sun,
we light for the party
pale candelabras in the dusty parlor,
and silence reveals to us the secret
we didn't want to hear.

Para hablar con los muertos

Para hablar con los muertos
hay que elegir palabras
que ellos reconozcan tan fácilmente
como sus manos
reconocían el pelaje de sus perros en la oscuridad.
Palabras claras y tranquilas
como el agua del torrente domesticada en la copa
o las sillas ordenadas por la madre
después que se han ido los invitados.
Palabras que la noche acoja
como a los fuegos fatuos los pantanos.

Para hablar con los muertos
hay que saber esperar:
ellos son miedosos
como los primeros pasos de un niño.
Pero si tenemos paciencia
un día nos responderán
con una hoja de álamo atrapada por un espejo roto,
con una llama de súbito reanimada en la chimenea,
con un regreso oscuro de pájaros
frente a la mirada de una muchacha
que aguarda inmóvil en el umbral.

To Talk with the Dead

To talk with the dead
you have to choose words
they can recognize as easily
as their hands recognized
their dog's fur in the darkness.
Words clear and calm
as the water of the torrent tamed in a cup
or the chairs rearranged by a mother
after all the guests have gone.
Words that night welcomes
as swamps welcome will-o'-the-wisps.

To talk with the dead
you have to know how to wait;
they are fearful
as the first steps of a child.
But if we have patience
one day they will answer us
with a poplar leaf trapped in a broken mirror,
with a flame that suddenly flares in the fireplace,
with a dark return of birds
before the glance of a girl
who waits motionless on the threshold.

Alegría

Centellean los rieles
pero nadie piensa en viajar.
De la sidreria viene olor
a manzanas recién molidas.
Sabemos que nunca estaremos solos
mientras haya un puñado de tierra fresca.

La llovizna es una oveja compasiva
lamiendo las heridas
hechas por el viento de invierno.
La sangre de las manzanas
ilumina la sidrería.

Desaparece la linterna roja
del último carro del tren.
Los vagabundos duermen
a la sombra de los tilos.
A nosotros nos basta mirar
un puñado de tierra en nuestras manos.

Es bueno beber un aso de cerveza
para prolongar la tarde.
Recordar el centelleo de los rieles.
Recordar la tristeza
dormida como una vieja sirvienta
en un rincón de la casa.
Contarles a los amigos desaparecidos
que afuera llueve en voz baja
y tener en las manos
un puñado de tierra fresca.

Happiness

The train tracks flash
but no one thinks of traveling.
Smell of apples recently crushed
comes from the cider press.
We know we will never be alone
so long as there's a handful of fresh earth.

The drizzle is a forlorn sheep
licking wounds
made by the winter wind.
Blood of the apples
lights up the cider press.

The red lantern
of the caboose disappears.
Tramps sleep in the shade of linden trees.
It's enough for us to look at
a handful of earth in our hands.

It's good to drink a glass of beer
to prolong the afternoon.
To remember the flash on the tracks.
To remember sadness
asleep like an old servant
in a corner of the house.
To tell our missing friends
that outside it is raining in a whisper
and to hold in our hands
a handful of fresh earth.

La llave

Dale la llave al otoño.
Háblale del río mudo en cuyo fondo
yace la sombra de los puentes de madera
desaparecidos hace muchos años.

No me has contado ninguno de tus secretos.
Pero tu mano es la llave que abre la puerta
del molino en ruinas donde duerme mi vida
entre polvo y más polvo,
y espectros de inviernos,
y los jinetes enlutados del viento
que huyen tras robar campanas
en las pobres aldeas.
Pero mis días serán nubes
para viajar por la primavera de tu cielo.

Saldremos en silencio,
sin despertar al tiempo.

Te diré que podremos ser felices.

The Key

Give the key to autumn.
Speak to it of the mute river in whose depth lies
the shadow of wooden bridges
gone for many years.

You haven't told me any of your secrets.
But your hand is the key that opens the door
of the ruined mill where my life sleeps
between dust and more dust,
and between ghosts of winters
and the mourning riders of the wind
who flee after stealing bells
in the poor towns.
But my days will be clouds
to travel through the spring of your sky.

We leave in silence,
without waking time.

I tell you we can be happy.

Estas palabras

Estas palabras quieren ser
un puñado de cerezas,
un susurro—¿para quién?—
entre una y otra oscuridad.

Sí, un puñado de cerezas,
un susurro—¿para quién?—
entre una y otra oscuridad.

These Words

These words want to be
a handful of cherries,
a whisper—for whom?—
between one darkness and another.

Yes, a handful of cherries,
a whisper—for whom?—
between one darkness and another.

Carta de lluvia

Si atraviesas las estaciones
conservando en tus manos
la lluvia de la infancia que debimos compartir
nos reuniremos en el lugar
donde los sueños corren jubilosos
como ovejas liberadas del corral
y en donde brillará sobre nosotros
la estrella que nos fuera prometida.

Pero ahora te envío esta carta de lluvia
que te lleva un jinete de lluvia
por caminos acostumbrados a la lluvia.

Ruega por mí, reloj,
en estas horas monótonas como ronroneos de gatos.
He vuelto al lugar que hace renacer
la ceniza de los fantasmas que odio.
Alguna vez salí al patio
a decirles a los conejos
que el amor había muerto.
Aquí no debo recordar a nadie.
Aquí debo olvidar los aromos
porque la mano que cortó aromos
ahora cava una fosa.

El pasto ha crecido demasiado.
En el techo de la casa vecina
se pudre una pelota de trapo
dejada por un niño muerto.
Entre las tablas del cerco
me vienen a mirar rostros que creía olvidados.
Mi amigo espera en vano que en el rio
centellee su buena estrella.

Letter of Rain

If you cross the seasons
holding in your hands
the rain of your childhood we should have shared
we will meet again in the place
where dreams run joyously
as sheep freed from the corral
and where the star we were promised
will shine above us.

But now I send you this letter of rain
that a rider of rain carries to you
by roads accustomed to rain.

Pray for me, clock,
in these hours monotonous as the purring of cats.
I have returned to the place
where the ash of ghosts I hate
is born again.
Once I went out to the patio
to tell the rabbits
love had died.
When I am here I shouldn't remember anyone.
When I am here I ought to forget the aromatic trees
because the hand that cut them
now digs a grave.

The pasture has grown too high.
On the roof of the neighboring house
a ball made of rags rots,
left there by a dead child.
Through the poles of the fence
faces I thought I'd forgotten come to look at me.
My friend waits in vain for his lucky star
to flash on the river.

Tú, como en mis sueños vienes
atravesando las estaciones,
con las lluvias de la infancia
en tus manos hechas cántaro.
En el invierno nos reunirá el fuego
que encenderemos juntos.
Nuestros cuerpos harán las noches tibias
como el aliento de los bueyes
y al despertar veré que el pan sobre la mesa
tiene un resplandor más grande que el de los planetas enemigos
cuando la partan tus manos de adolescente.

Pero ahora te envío una carta de lluvia
que te lleva un jinete de lluvia
por caminos acostumbrados a la lluvia.

You—as if in my dreams—
come crossing the seasons,
with the rains of childhood
in your cupped hands.
In the winter the fire we light together
will unite us.
Our bodies will make nights warm
as the breath of oxen
and on waking I will see that the bread on the table
has a greater dazzle than enemy planets
when your young hands break it.

But now I send you a letter of rain
that a rider of rain carries to you
by roads accustomed to rain.

II

When Everyone Leaves

Cuando todos se vayan

a Eduardo Molina Ventura

Cuando todos se vayan a otros planetas
yo quedaré en la ciudad abandonada
bebiendo un último vaso de cerveza,
y luego volveré al pueblo donde siempre regreso
como el borracho a la taberna
y el niño a cabalgar
en el balancín roto.

Y en el pueblo no tendré nada que hacer,
sino echarme luciérnagas a los bolsillos
o caminar a orillas de rieles oxidados
o sentarme en el roído mostrador de un almacén
para hablar con antiguos compañeros de escuela.

Como una araña que recorre
los mismos hilos de su red
caminaré sin prisa por las calles
invadidas de malezas
mirando los palomares
que se vienen abajo,
hasta llegar a mi casa
donde me encerraré a escuchar
discos de un cantante de 1930
sin cuidarme jamás de mirar
los caminos infinitos
trazados por los cohetes en el espacio.

When Everyone Leaves

To Eduardo Molina Ventura
in memoriam 1913–1986

When everyone leaves for other planets
I will stay behind in the abandoned city
drinking a last glass of beer,
and then I will return to the town to which I always return
as the drunk returns to his tavern
and the child comes back to straddle
a broken crossbeam.

And in the town I'll have nothing to do,
except put fireflies in my pockets
or walk on the edge of rusty rails
or sit down on the dilapidated store counter
to talk with old pals from school.

Like a spider that travels over and over
the same threads of its net
I will walk slowly through streets
invaded by thickets
looking at the pigeon coops
that are falling down,
until I get to my house
where I will shut myself up to listen
to records of a singer from the thirties
never caring to watch
the infinite roads
traced by rockets in space.

Cuento de la tarde

Es tarde,
El tren del norte ha pasado.
En tu casa la cena se enfría,
las madejas ruedan
desde la falda de tu madre dormida.
He estado inmóvil mientras hablabas.
La palabras no son nada
junto a la hoja que resucita al pasar frente a tu cara,
junto al barco de papel
que me enseñaste a hacer.
No he mirado sino tu reflejo en el estanque.

Es tarde.
Las horas son madejas rodando
desde la falda de tu madre dormida.
Volvamos al pueblo.
Las ranas repiten inútilmente su mensaje.
Te ayudo a saltar un charco, te muestro un vagabundo
encendiendo fuego en un galpón abandonado.
Estrellas irreales hacen extinguirse
las miedosas sonrisas de los tejados rojizos.
Nada debe existir.
Nada sino nuestros inmóviles reflejos
que aún retiene el estanque
y esas hojas
a veces resucitadas al pasar frente a tu cara.

Story of the Afternoon

It is late.
The train to the north has gone by.
In your house supper is getting cold,
skeins fall
from the lap of your sleeping mother.
I have kept still while you talked.
Words are nothing
beside the leaf that comes to life when it passes before your face,
beside the paper boat
you taught me to make.
I have looked only at your reflection in the pool.

It is late.
The hours are skeins falling
from the lap of your sleeping mother.
Let's go back to town.
The frogs uselessly repeat their message.
I'll help you jump a puddle, I'll show you a tramp
lighting a fire in an abandoned shack.
Unreal stars extinguish
the frightened smiles of the red roofs.
Nothing ought to exist.
Nothing but our unmoving reflection
still retained by the pool
and those leaves that sometimes come to life
when they pass before your face.

La última isla

De nuevo vida y muerte se confunden
como en el patio de la casa
la entrada de las carretas
con el ruido del balde en el pozo.
De nuevo el cielo recuerda con odio
la herida del relámpago,
y los almendros no quieren pensar
en sus negras raíces.

El silencio no puede seguir siendo mi lenguaje,
pero sólo encuentro esas palabras irreales
que los muertos les dirigen a los astros y a las hormigas,
y de mi memoria desaparecen el amor y la alegría
como la luz de una jarra de agua
lanzada inútilmente contra las tinieblas.

De nuevo sólo se escucha
el crepitar inextinguible de la lluvia
que cae y cae sin saber por qué,
parecida a la anciana solitaria que sigue
tejiendo y tejiendo;
y se quiere huir hacia un pueblo
donde un trompo todavía no deja de girar
esperando que yo lo recoja,
pero donde se ponen los pies
desaparecen los caminos,
y es mejor quedarse inmóvil en este cuarto
pues quizás ha llegado el término del mundo,
y la lluvia es el estéril eco de ese fin,
una canción que tratan de recordar
labios que se deshacen bajo tierra.

The Last Island

Again life and death get mixed up
as in the courtyard of the house
the entry of the carts
mixes with the noise of the bucket in the well.
Again heaven remembers with hate
the lightning wound,
and the almond trees don't want to think
about their black roots.

Silence can't go on being my language,
but I can find only those unreal words
the dead address to stars and ants,
and love and happiness disappear from my memory
like light from a pitcher of water
thrown uselessly against the darkness.

Again you can hear only
the inextinguishable pattering of rain
that falls and falls without knowing why,
just as the lonely old woman goes on
weaving and weaving;
and you want to run away to a town
where a top still doesn't stop whirling,
waiting for me to pick it up,
but wherever you put your feet,
the roads disappear,
and it is better to remain motionless in this room,
since maybe the end of the world has come,
and the rain is the sterile echo of that end,
a song that a mouth decomposing in the earth
is trying to remember.

Carta

Cuando al fin te des cuenta
que sólo puedo amar los pueblos
donde nunca se detienen los trenes,
ya podrás olvidarme
para saber quien soy de veras.

Sabrás quien soy de veras
y los anillos de la corteza del árbol
serán señal de nuestros desposales,
y podrás entrar al bosque
donde te hallé antes de conocerte.

Y el bosque donde te hallé sin conocerte
se llenará con las hojas de mis palabras.
La noche será luminosa de ojos de caballos
que vienen a beber las aguas del recuerdo
para que siempre haya un amor que no muere.

Porque siempre hay en mí un amor que no muere
y eso te lo dirán los pueblos donde el tren no se detiene,
y el guitarrista ebrio
que entona la canción que te escribí
hará detenerse el remolino de las calles
para mostrarte el camino hacia el bosque.

Letter

When at last you realize
I can love only those towns
where the trains never stop,
then you will be able to forget me
in order to know who I truly am.

You will know who I truly am
and rings made from tree bark
will be the token of our wedding vows,
and you will be able to enter the forest
where I found you before I met you.

And the forest where I found you without knowing you
will fill up with the leaves of my words.
Night will be luminous with the eyes of horses
come to drink the waters of memory
so there will always be a love that doesn't die.

Because there is always in me a love that doesn't die
and the towns where the train doesn't stop
will tell you this, while the drunk guitar player
who croons the song I wrote you
will have to stop the whirling of the streets
to show you the road into the forest.

Camino rural

Solitario camino rural
a fines del verano.
¿Qué puedo hacer
troncos podridos sobre el charco?
Temo llegar al pueblo
cuando la niebla se desprende de la tierra.
Temo llegar al pueblo
porque a otro esperan allí
las mujeres que duermen en montones de heno.
Para otro van a amasar pan las hermanas esta noche.
Para otro contarán historias
los que encienden hogueras en los barbechos.

Aparecen lejanas luces
como débiles tañidos de guitarras.
Las perdices silban
llamando a sus parejas.
El pozo se aniega de hojas de castaños.
Alguien cierra las ventanas
para no sentir el cruel olor
a glicinas de otro verano.
Salen estrellas desesperadas
como abejas que no pueden hallar el colmenar.

¡Adiós, troncos podridos sobre el charco!
Voy hacia un pueblo donde nadie me espera
por un solitario carmino rural
a fines del verano.

Country Road

Lonely country road
at the end of summer.
What can I make
of rotten trunks over the puddle?

I am afraid of arriving at the town
when mist is rising from the earth.
I am afraid of arriving at the town
because there women who sleep on piles of hay
wait for someone else.
For someone else, the sisters are going to make bread tonight.
For someone else, those who light bonfires in the fallow fields
will tell stories.

Distant lights appear
like the weak strumming of guitars.
Quails whistle,
calling to their mates.
The well is drowning in chestnut leaves.
Someone closes the windows
to keep from smelling the cruel odor
of wisterias from another summer.
The desperate stars come out
like bees that can't find their hive.

Good-bye, rotten trunks over the puddle!
I am headed for a town where nobody waits for me
by way of a lonely country road
at the end of summer.

Después de todo

Después de todo
nos volveremos a encontrar.
El verano tenderá sus manteles en el suelo
para que dispongamos nuestras provisiones
y tú seguirás bella
como la canción *El Vino de Mediodía*
que el loco tocaba en la leñera.

Después de todo
hay tantas y tantas tierras.
Yo no me impaciento.
Tenemos todos los años del mundo para recorrerlas
hasta que de nuevo estemos juntos
y tú me contarás
que una vez me conociste
en un pequeño planeta que yo no recuerdo
un planeta llamado Tierra
y vas a hablarme
de casas visitadas por la luna,
billetes de apuesta a los hipódromos,
nuestras iniciales dibujadas con tiza blanca en un muro en demolición.

Equivoquémonos todo lo que queramos.
La tierra del desamor no existe
ante el gesto tuyo de mostrar las magnolias de una plaza de barrio,
tu cabeza en mi hombro,
la clara música nocturna de tu cuerpo.
Un gesto rehace todo:
Cuando la casa se incendia
su vida sigue entera
en la hoja chamuscada de un cuaderno,
el alfil sobreviviente del ajedrez.

After All

After all
we will meet again.
Summer will spread its tablecloth over the ground
so we can set out our provisions
and you will still be as beautiful
as the song "Noon Wine"
the crazy man used to play in the woodshed.

After all
there are so many, many lands.
I'm not feeling impatient.
We have all the years of the world to travel them
until we will be together again
and you will tell me
you knew me once
on a little planet I don't remember,
a planet called Earth,
and you will speak to me
of houses visited by the moon,
betting at the racetracks,
our initials drawn with white chalk on a wall being torn down.

Let us make as many mistakes as we like.
The land of love-no-more doesn't exist
before your gesture as you point out magnolias in a neighborhood
        plaza,
your head on my shoulder,
the clear nocturnal music of your body.
A gesture mends everything:
When the house burns up
its life continues whole
in the singed leaf of a notebook,
the surviving bishop of the chess set.

En otro lugar,
lejos de esta tierra y de su tiempo
espero tu rostro
donde se reúnen todos los rostros que he amado,
y comenzaremos a ser otra vez los desconocidos
que hace años se miraban y miraban
sin atreverse a decir que iban a amarse.

In another place,
far from this earth and from its time,
I wait for your face
where all the faces I have loved will meet,
and we will begin again to be strangers
who years ago gazed at each other and gazed
not daring to say they were about to fall in love.

Andenes

Te gusta llegar a la estación
cuando el reloj de pared tictaquea,
tictaquea en la oficina del jefe-estación.
Cuando la tarde cierra sus párpados
de viajera fatigada
y los rieles ya se pierden
bajo el hollín de la oscuridad.

Te gusta quedarte en la estación desierta
cuando no puedes abolir la memoria,
como las nubes de vapor
los contornos de las locomotoras,
y te gusta ver pasar al viento
que silba como un vagabundo
aburrido de caminar sobre los rieles.

Tictaqueo del reloj. Ves de nuevo
los pueblos cuyos nombres nunca aprendiste,
el pueblo donde querías llegar
como al niño el día de su cumpleaños
y los viajes de vuelta de vacaciones
cuando eras—para los parientes que te esperaban-
sólo un alumno fracasado con olor a cerveza.

Tictaqueo del reloj. El jefe-estación
juega un solitario. El reloj sigue diciendo
que la noche es el único tren
que puede llegar a este pueblo,
y a tí te gusta estar inmóvil escuchándolo
mientras el hollín de la oscuridad
hace desaparecer los durmientes de la vía.

Platforms

You like to get to the station
when the wall clock ticktocks,
ticktocks in the office of the stationmaster.
When the afternoon shuts its eyelids
like a tired traveler
and the tracks get lost
beneath the soot of darkness.

You like to stay in the empty station
when you can't obscure memory
the way clouds of steam
obscure the outline of locomotives,
and you like to see the wind pass
whistling like a tramp
bored with walking the rails.

Ticktock of the clock. You see again
the towns whose names you never learned,
the town at which you wanted to arrive
as a boy longs to reach the day of his birthday,
and the trips returning from vacations
when you were—for the relatives who waited for you—
only a student, flunking, reeking of beer.

Ticktock of the clock. The stationmaster
plays solitaire. The clock goes on saying
night is the only train
that can arrive at this town,
and it pleases you to stand still listening to it
while the soot of darkness
makes the ties disappear from the track.

III
The Land of Night

Cuento sobre una rama de mirto

Había una vez una muchacha
que amaba dormir en el lecho de un río.
Y sin temor pascaba por el bosque
porque llevaba en la mano
una jaula con un grillo guardián.

Para esperarla yo me convertía
en la casa de madera de sus antepasados
alzada a orillas de un brumoso lago.
Las puertas y las ventanas siempre estaban abiertas
pero sólo nos visitaba su primo el Porquerizo
que nos traia de regalo
perezosos gatos
que a veces abrian sus ojos
para que viéran os pasar por sus pupilas
cortejos de bodas campesinas.
El sacerdote había muerto
y todo ramo de mirto se marchitaba.

Teníamos tres hijas
descalzas y silenciosas como la belladona.
Todas las mañanas recogían helechos
y nos hablaron sólo para decirnos
que un jinete las llevaría
a ciudades cuyos nombres nunca conoceríamos.

Pero nos revelaron el conjuro
con el cual las abejas
sabrían que éramos sus amos
y el molino
nos daría trigo
sin permiso del viento.

Nosotros esperamos a nuestros hijos
crueles y fascinantes
como halcones en el puño del cazador.

Story about a Branch of Myrtle

Once upon a time there was a girl
who loved to sleep in the bed of a river.
And she went rambling fearless through the forest
because she carried in her hand
a guardian cricket in a cage.

Waiting for her I changed myself
into the wooden house of her ancestors
high on the shores of a misty lake.
My doors and windows were always open
but the only one who visited us was her cousin Swineherd,
who brought us a gift of lazy cats
which sometimes opened their eyes
so we could see
the processions of country weddings
passing across their pupils.
The priest had died
and every branch of myrtle withered.

We had three daughters
barefoot and silent as belladonna.
Every morning they gathered ferns
and only spoke to us to say
a rider would carry them off
to cities whose names we'd never know.

But they revealed the spells to us
that would teach the bees
we were their masters
and make the mill
give us wheat
without the wind's permission.

We waited for our children,
cruel and fascinating
as falcons on the hunter's fist.

Bajo un viejo techo

Esta noche duermo bajo un viejo techo,
los ratones corren sobre él, como hace mucho tiempo,
y el niño que hay en mí renace en mi sueño,
aspira de nuevo el olor de los muebles de roble,
y mira lleno de miedo hacia la ventana,
pues sabe que ninguna estrella resucita.

Esa noche oí caer las nueces desde el nogal,
escuché los consejos del reloj de péndulo,
supe que el viento vuelca una copa del cielo,
que las sombras se extienden
y la tierra las bebe sin amarlas,
pero el árbol de mi sueño sólo daba hojas verdes
que maduraban en la mañana con el canto del gallo.

Esta noche duermo bajo un viejo techo,
los ratones corren sobre él, como hace mucho tiempo,
pero sé que no hay mañanas y no hay cantos de gallos,
abro los ojos, para no ver reseco el árbol de mis sueños,
y bajo él, la muerte que me tiende la mano.

Under an Old Roof

Tonight I sleep under an old roof,
mice run over it as they did long ago,
and the child who lives in me is reborn in my dreams,
breathes again the odor of oak furniture,
and looks toward the window full of fear,
since he knows no star ever comes back to life.

That night I heard the walnuts fall from the tree,
I listened to the advice of the grandfather clock,
I learned that the wind tips the sky's cup over,
shadows spill out
and earth drinks them without loving them,
but the tree of my dreams bore only green leaves
that grew in the morning when the rooster crowed.

Tonight I sleep under an old roof,
mice run over it as they did long ago,
but I know there are no mornings and no roosters crowing.
I open my eyes, in order not to see the tree of my dreams withered,
and under it, death holding out her hand to me.

La tierra de la noche

No hablemos.
Es mejor abrir las ventanas mudas
desde la muerte de la hermana mayor.

La voz de la hierba hace callar la noche:
Hace un mes no llueve.
Nidos vacíos caen desde la enredadera.
Los cerezos se apagan como añejas canciones.
Este mes será de los muertos.
Este mes será del espectro
de la luna de verano.

Sigue brillando, luna de verano.
Reviven los escalones de piedra
gastados por los pasos de los antepasados.
Los murciélagos no dejan de chillar
entre los muros ruinosos de la Cervecería.
El azadón roto
espera tierra fresca de nuevas tumbas.
Y nosotros no debemos hablar
cuando la luna brilla
más blanca y despiadada que los huesos de los muertos.

Sigue brillando, luna de verano.

The Land of Night

Let's not talk.
It's better to open windows
mute since the death of the oldest sister.

The voice of the grass makes night hush:
It hasn't rained for a month.
Empty nests fall from the vine.
The cherry trees go out like vintage songs.
This month will be for the dead.
This month will be for the ghost
of the summer moon.

Shine on, summer moon.
Stone stairs worn down
by the steps of ancestors come alive.
Bats don't stop chittering
among the crumbling walls of the Brewery.
The broken hoe
waits for fresh earth from new graves.
And we shouldn't speak
when the moon shines
whiter and more merciless than the bones of the dead.

Shine on, summer moon.

Sentados frente al fuego

Sentados frente al fuego que envejece
miro su rostro sin decir palabra.
Miro el jarro de greda donde aún queda vino,
miro nuestras sombras movidas por las llamas.

Esta es la misma estación que descubrimos juntos,
a pesar de su rostro frente al fuego,
y de nuestras sombras movidas por las llamas.
Quizás si yo pudiera encontrar una palabra.

Esta es la misma estación que descubrimos juntos:
aún cae una gotera, brilla el cerezo tras la lluvia.
Pero nuestras sombras movidas por las llamas
viven más que nosotros.

Si, ésta es la misma estación que descubrimos juntos:
—Yo llenaba esas manos de cerezas, esas
manos llenaban mi vaso de vino—.
Ella mira el fuego que envejece.

Sitting in Front of the Fire

Sitting in front of the fire that is growing old
I look at her face without saying a word.
I look at the cup in which wine still remains,
I look at our shadows moved by flames.

This is the season we discovered together,
in spite of her face before the fire
and our shadows moved by flames.
Perhaps if I could find a word. . . .

This is the season we discovered together:
a drizzle still falls, the cherry tree shines through rain.
But our shadows moved by flames
are more alive than we are.

Yes, this is the season we discovered together—
I filled those hands with cherries,
those hands filled my glass with wine.
She looks at the fire that is growing old.

Puente en el sur

Ayer he recordado un día de claro invierno. He recordado
un puente sobre el río, un río robándole azul al cielo.
Mi amor era menos que nada en ese puente. Una naranja
hundiéndose en las aguas, una voz que no sabe a quién llama,
una gaviota cuyo brillo se deshizo entre los pinos.

Ayer he recordado que no se es nadie sobre un puente
cuando el invierno sueña con la claridad de otra estación,
y se quiere ser una hoja inmóvil en el sueño del invierno,
y el amor es menos que una naranja perdiéndose en las aguas,
menos que una gaviota cuya luz se extingue entre los pinos.

Bridge in the South

Yesterday I remembered a day of clear winter. I remembered
a bridge over the river, a river stealing blue from the sky.
On that bridge my love was less than nothing: an orange
sinking in the water, a voice that doesn't know whom it calls,
a gull whose shine dissolved among the pines.

Yesterday I remembered one isn't anyone on a bridge
when winter dreams of the clarity of another season,
and one wants to be a still leaf in winter's dream,
and love is less than an orange sinking in the water,
less than a sea gull whose light goes out among pines.

Día de feria

a Jorge Aravena Llanca

Día de feria
frente a las figuras de greda:
frente a esas luces
encendidas por dedos morenos que cambiaban por ellas
la sopa caliente, el pedazo de pan.
Y en el día de feria
estas figuras de greda
están mucho más vivas
que las miradas impasibles de quienes no las comprenden,
que las vanas monedas, que las campanadas que cruzan la plaza.
Viven hechas sangre en nuestra sangre, como el vaso de vino tinto,
la charla de invierno junto a los rescoldos,
—eso que está en nosotros
más que el miedo en la noche.

Yo había conocido antes esta certeza,
esta alegría humilde,
sí: unas flores silvestres creciendo entre los rieles,
bautizos donde los padrinos
no tenían dinero que lanzar al aire.
Pero sólo ahora sé
que he crecido para ellas:
manos de campesinos, terrones pardos y fecundos
para que el oro vuelva a su lugar
y el hierro no sea más una herramienta de sepultureros.
Y entre la multitud del día de feria respiro un aire puro
libre de cánticos para muertos.

Fair Day

To Jorge Aravena Llanca

Fair day
in front of the clay statues:
in front of these candles
lit by dark fingers that gave up
hot soup, a piece of bread, to light them.
And on fair day
these figures of clay are much more alive
than the impassive glances of people
who don't understand them,
than useless coins, than bells tolling across the plaza.
They live blood in our blood, like red wine,
winter conversation beside the embers—
whatever is greater in us
than fear of the dark.

I had known this certainty before,
this humble happiness,
yes: some wild flowers growing between the rails,
baptisms where the godparents
didn't have money to toss into the air.
Only now do I know
I have grown up for these things:
peasant hands, dark and fertile clods of soil,
so that gold may return to its place
and iron be only a gravedigger's tool.
And among the multitude on fair day I breathe a pure air
free of canticles for the dead.

Sin señal de vida

¿Para qué dar señales de vida?
Apenas podría enviarte con el mozo
un mensaje en una servilleta.

Aunque no estés aquí.

Aunque estés a años sombra de distancia
te amo de repente
a las tres de la tarde,
la hora en que los locos
sueñan con ser espantapájaros vestidos de marineros
espantando nubes en los trigales.

No sé si recordarte
es un acto de desesperación o elegancia
en un mundo donde al fin
el único sacramento ha llegado a ser el suicidio.

Tal vez habría que cambiar la palanca del cruce
para que se descarrilen los trenes.
Hacer el amor
en el único Hotel del pueblo
para oír rechinar los molinos de agua
e interrumpir la siesta del teniente de carabineros
y del oficial del Registro Civil.

Si caigo preso por ebriedad o toque de queda
hazme señas de sol con tu espejo de mano
frente al cual te empolvas
como mis compañeras de tiempo de Liceo.

Not a Sign of Life

Denmark is a prison.
—*Hamlet*

Why give signs of life?
I could hardly send you a message
in a napkin with the waiter.

Even though you aren't here.
Even though you are shadow years away,
I love you suddenly
at three in the afternoon,
the hour when madmen
dream of being scarecrows dressed in sailor suits
frightening clouds in the wheatfields.

I don't know if remembering you
is an act of despair or elegance
in a world where at last
suicide has become the only sacrament.

Perhaps I would have to throw the switch at the crossing
to derail the trains.
To make love
in the only Hotel in town
in order to hear the water mills grind
and interrupt the nap of the police lieutenant
and the clerk at the Civil Registry.

If I land in jail for drinking or breaking the curfew,
send me sun signs with the hand mirror
you use when you powder your face
as my girlfriends from high-school days once did.

Y no te entretengas
en enseñarle palabras feas a los choroyes.
Enséñales sólo a decir Papá o Centro de Madres.
Acuérdate que estamos en un tiempo donde se habla en voz baja,
y sorber la sopa un día de Banquete de Gala
significa soñar en voz alta.

Qué hermoso es el tiempo de la austeridad.
Las esposas cantan felices
mientras zurcen el terno único
del marido cesante.

Ya nunca más correrá sangre por las calles.
Los roedores están comiendo nuestro queso
en nombre de un futuro
donde todas las cacerolas
estarán rebosantes de sopa,
y los camiones vacilarán bajo el peso del alba.

Aprende a portarte bien
en un país donde la delación será una virtud.
Aprende a viajar en globo
y lanza por la borda todo tu lastre:
Los discos de Joan Baez, Bob Dylan, los Quilapayún,
aprende de memoria los Quincheros y el 7° de Línea.
Olvida las enseñanzas del Niño de Chocolate, Gurdgieff o el Grupo Arica,
quema la autobiografía de Trotzki o la de Freud
o los 20 *Poemas de Amor* en edición firmada y numerada por el autor.

Acuérdate que no me gustan las artesanías
ni dormir en una carpa en la playa.
Y nunca te hubiese querido más
que a los suplementos deportivos de los lunes.

And don't waste time
teaching dirty words to the parrots.
Teach them only to say "Papa" or "The Mothers' Club."
Remember we live in a time when you must speak in a whisper,
and sipping soup one day at the Awards Banquet
means to dream aloud.

How beautiful is the time of austerity.
Wives sing happily
while they darn the only suit
owned by their unemployed husbands.

Nevermore will blood run through our streets.
The rats are eating our cheese
in the name of a future
where all the pots and pans
will be overflowing with soup,
and the trucks will wobble under the weight of dawn.

Learn how to behave well
in a country where denunciation will be a virtue.
Learn how to travel in a balloon
and toss all your ballast overboard.
Learn by heart the records of Joan Baez, Bob Dylan,
the Quilapayún, the Quincheros, and the 7th Regiment.
Forget the teachings of Chocolate Boy, Gurdjieff, or the Arica Group,
burn the autobiographies of Trotsky and Freud
and *Twenty Love Poems* in an edition
signed and numbered by the author.

Remember I don't like handicrafts
or sleeping in a tent on the beach.
And never could I have loved you more
than the Monday sports supplement.

Y no sigas pensando en los atardeceres en los bosques.
En mi provincia prohibieron hasta el paso de los gitanos.

Y ahora
voy a pedir otro jarrito de chicha con naranja
y tú
mejor enciérrate en un convento.
Estoy leyendo *El Grito de Guerra* del Ejército de Salvación.

Dicen que la sífilis de nuevo será incurable
y que nuestros hijos pueden soñar en ser economistas o dictadores.

And don't go on thinking about afternoons in the forest.
In my part of the country they have forbidden the gypsies even
      to pass through.

And now
I'm going to order another cup
of *chicha* with orange juice

and you'd
better close yourself up in a convent.
I'm reading *The War Cry* of the Salvation Army.
They say syphilis will again be incurable,
and our children can dream of becoming economists or dictators.

IV

I Would Give All the Gold in the World

Daría todo el oro del mundo

Daría todo el oro del mundo
por sentir de nuevo en mi camisa
las frías monedas de la lluvia.

Por oír rodar el aro de alambre
en que un niño descalzo
lleva el sol a un puente.

Por ver aparecer
caballos y cometas
en los sitios vacíos de mi juventud.

Por oler otra vez
los buenos hijos de la harina
que oculta bajo su delantal la mesa.

Para gustar
la leche del alba
que va llenando los pozos olvidados.

Daria no sé cuánto
por descansar en la tierra
con las frías monedas de plata de la lluvia
cerrándome los ojos.

I Would Give All the Gold in the World

I would give all the gold in the world
to feel the cold coins of rain
again on my shirt.

To hear the rolling of the wire hoop
in which a barefoot child
carries the sun to a bridge.

To see
horses and kites appear
in the wide-open places of my youth.

To smell once more
the good offspring of the flour
who hides the table under her apron.

To taste
the milk of dawn
gradually filling forgotten wells.

I would give I don't know how much
to lie down on the ground
with the cold silver coins of rain
closing my eyes.

Regalo

Un amigo del sur
me ha enviado una manzana
demasiado hermosa
para comerla de inmediato.
La tengo en mis manos:
es pesada y redonda
como la Tierra.

Gift

A friend from the South
has sent me an apple
too beautiful
to eat right away.
I hold it in my hands:
It is heavy and round
like the Earth.

Poema de invierno

El invierno trae caballos blancos que resbalan en la helada.
Han encendido fuego para defender los huertos
de la bruja blanca de la helada.
Entre la blanca humareda se agita el cuidador.
El perro entumecido amenaza desde su caseta al témpano flotante de
la luna.

Esta noche al niño se le perdonará que duerma tarde.
En las casa los padres están de fiesta.
Pero él abre las ventanas
para ver a los enmascarados jinetes
que lo esperan en el bosque
y sabe que su destino
será amar el olor humilde de los senderos nocturnos.

El invierno trae aguardiente para el maquinista y el fogonero.
Una estrella perdida tambalea como baliza.
Cantos de soldados ebrios
que vuelven tarde a sus cuarteles.

En la casa ha empezado la fiesta.
Pero el niño sabe que la fiesta está en otra parte,
y mira por la ventana buscando a los desconocidos
que pasará toda la vida tratando de encontrar.

Winter Poem

Winter brings white horses that skid on the ice.
Someone's lit a fire to protect the gardens
from the white witch of ice.
Among white puffs of smoke the caretaker frets.
From his doghouse, the numb dog menaces the floating drum
    of the moon.

Tonight the child will be pardoned for sleeping late.
In the house the parents are celebrating.
But the child opens the windows
to see the masked riders
who wait for him in the forest
and he knows his destiny will be
to love the damp odor of night paths.

Winter brings *aguardiente* for the machinist and the stoker.
A lost star reeling like a buoy.
Songs of tipsy soldiers
returning late to their barracks.

In the house the party has begun.
But the child knows the party is somewhere else
and he looks out the window searching for the strangers
he will spend his whole life trying to find.

Fin del mundo

El día del fin del mundo
será limpio y ordenado
como el cuaderno del mejor alumno.
El borracho del pueblo
dormirá en una zanja,
el tren expreso pasará
sin detenerse en la estación,
y la banda del Regimiento
ensayará infinitamente
la marcha que toca hace veinte años en la plaza.
Sólo que algunos niños
dejarán sus volantines enredados
en los alambres telefónicos,
para volver llorando a sus casas
sin saber qué decir a sus madres
y yo grabaré mis iniciales
en la corteza de un tilo
pensando que eso no sirve para nada.

Los evangélicos saldrán a las esquinas
a cantar sus himnos de costumbre.
La anciana loca paseará con su quitasol.
Y yo diré:»El mundo no puede terminar
porque las palomas y los gorriones
siguen peleando por la avena en el patio«.

End of the World

The day of the end of the world
will be as clean and orderly
as the notebook of the best student.
The town drunk
will sleep in a ditch,
the express train will go by
without stopping at the station,
and the Regimental band
will practice infinitely
the march it played in the plaza twenty years ago.
Only, some children
will leave their tangled string
in the telephone wires
to run home crying
without knowing what to say to their mothers,
and I will carve my initials
in the bark of a linden
thinking it will do no good.

The evangelicals will come out to the corners
to sing their usual hymns.
The crazy old lady will parade with her parasol.
And I will say: "The world can't end
because the pigeons and sparrows
are still fighting for oats in the patio."

Imagen para un estanque

Y así pasan las tardes:
silenciosas, como gastadas monedas
en manos de avaros.
Y yo escribo cartas que nunca envío
mientras los manzanos se extinguen
víctimas de sus propias llamas.

Hasta que de lejos
vienen las voces
de ventanas golpeadas por el viento
en las casas desiertas,
y pasan bueyes desenyugados
que van a beber al estero.
Entonces debo pedirle al tiempo
un recuerdo que no se deforme
en el turbio estanque de la memoria.

Y horas que sean
reflejos de sol
en el dedal de la hermana,
crepitar de la leña
quemándose en la chimenea
y claros guijarros
lanzados al río por un ciego.

Image for a Pool

And so the afternoons pass:
silent, like worn coins
in misers' hands.
And I write letters I never send
while the apple trees die out,
victims of their own flame.

Until from far away
voices come
from windows in deserted houses
battered by wind,
and oxen pass unyoked,
going to drink at the water hole.
Then I should ask of time
one recollection that isn't deformed
in the murky pool of memory.

And hours may be
reflections of sun
on my sister's thimble,
cracklings of wood
burning in the fireplace,
and shining pebbles
skipped on the river by a blind man.

Edad de oro

Un día u otro
todos seremos felices.
Yo estaré libre
de mi sombra y mi nombre.
El que tuvo temor
escuchará junto a los suyos
los pasos de su madre,
el rostro de la amada será siempre joven
al reflejo de la luz antigua en la ventana,
y el padre hallará en la despensa la linterna
para buscar en el patio
la navaja extraviada.

No sabremos
si la caja de música
suena durante horas o un minuto;
tú hallarás—sin sorpresa—
el atlas sobre el cual soñaste con extraños países,
tendrás en tus manos
un pez venido del río de tu pueblo,
y Ella alzará sus párpados
y será de nuevo pura y grave
como las piedras lavadas por la lluvia.

Todos nos reuniremos
bajo la solemne y aburrida mirada
de personas que nunca han existido,
y nos saludaremos sonriendo apenas
pues todavía creeremos estar vivos.

Golden Age

One day or another
we will all be happy.
I will be free
of my shadow and my name.
The one who was afraid
will hear in his own footsteps
the steps of his mother,
the face of the loved one will be forever young
in the reflection of old light from the window,
and the father will find his flashlight in the pantry
so he can search for the hidden pocketknife
in the patio.

We won't know
if the music box
plays for hours or a minute;
you will discover—without surprise—
the atlas that made you dream of strange countries,
you will hold in your hands
a fish pulled from the river in your hometown,
and She will open her eyes wide
and be once again pure and grave
as stones washed by rain.

We will all be reunited
beneath the solemn and bored gaze
of people who have never existed,
and we will greet each other barely smiling,
because we will still believe we are alive.

Despedida

. . . el caso no ofrece
ningún adorno para la diadema de las Musas.

—*Ezra Pound*

Me despido de mi mano
que pudo mostrar el paso del rayo
o la quietud de las piedras
bajo las nievas de antaño.

Para que vuelvan a ser bosques y arenas
me despido del papel blanco y de la tinta azul
de donde surgían los ríos perezosos,
cerdos en las calles, molinos vacíos.

Me despido de los amigos
en quienes más he confiado:
los conejos y las polillas,
las nubes harapientas del verano.

Me despido de las Virtudes y de las Gracias del planeta:
Los fracasados, las cajas de música,
los murciélagos que al atardecer se deshojan
de los bosques de las casas de madera.

Me despido de los amigos silenciosos
a los que sólo les importa saber
dónde se puede beber algo de vino,
y para los cuales todos los días
no son sino un pretexto
para entonar canciones pasadas de moda.

Me despido de una muchacha
que sin preguntarme si la amaba o no la amaba
caminó conmigo y se acostó conmigo
cualquiera tarde de esas que se llenan
de humaredas de hojas quemándose en las aceras.

Good-bye

... the case presents
No adjunct to the Muses' diadem.
　　　　—*Ezra Pound*

I say good-bye to my hand,
which could move as fast as lightning
or lie still as stones
beneath the snows of yesteryear.

So they can become forests and sands again,
I say good-bye to white paper and blue ink
from which lazy rivers used to grow,
pigs in the street, empty mills.

I say good-bye to the friends
I've trusted most:
rabbits and moths,
tattered clouds of summer.

I say good-bye to the Virtues and Graces of this planet:
failures, music boxes,
bats that defoliate the forests
of wooden houses at dusk.

I say good-bye to silent friends,
those who only want to know
where we can go to drink some wine,
and for whom every day
is nothing but a pretext
for crooning songs long out of fashion.

I say good-bye to a girl
who never asked me whether I loved her or not
but walked with me and went to bed with me
on any of those afternoons filled
with the smoke of leaves burning on the sidewalk.

Me despido de una muchacha
cuya cara suelo ver en sueños
iluminada por la triste mirada
de linternas de trenes que parten hacia la lluvia.

Me despido de la memoria
y me despido de la nostalgia
—la sal y el agua
de mis días sin objeto—

y me despido de estos poemas:
palabras, palabras—un poco de aire
movido por los labios—palabras
para ocultar quizás lo único verdadero:
que respiramos y dejamos de respirar.

I say good-bye to a girl
whose face I usually see in dreams
lit up by the sad flash
of train lights departing in the rain.

I say good-bye to memory
and I say good-bye to nostalgia—
salt and water
of my aimless days—

and I say good-bye to these poems:
words, words—a little bit of air
stirred by my lips—words
to hide, perhaps, the only truth:
we breathe and we stop breathing.

Wesleyan Poetry in Translation

from Arabic

Desert Tracings: Six Classic Arabian Odes by ʿAlqama, Shánfara, Labid, ʿAntara, Al-Aʿsha, and Dhu al-Rúmma. 1989. Translated and introduced by Michael A. Sells.

from Bulgarian

Because the Sea Is Black: Poems of Blaga Dimitrova. 1989. Translated and with introductions by Niko Boris and Heather McHugh.

from Chinese

Bright Moon, Perching Bird: Poems by Li Po and Tu Fu. 1987. Translated and with an introduction by J. P. Seaton and James Cryer.

from Czechoslovakian

Mirroring: Selected Poems of Vladimír Holan. 1985. Translated by C. G. Hanzlicek and Dana Hábová.

from French

Fables from Old French: Aesop's Beasts and Bumpkins. 1982. Translated and with a preface by Norman Shapiro; introduction by Howard Needler.

The Book of Questions (Vols. I–VII in four books). 1976, 1977, 1983, 1984. By Edmond Jabès. Translated by Rosmarie Waldrop.

The Book of Dialogue. 1987. By Edmond Jabès. Translated by Rosmarie Waldrop.

The Book of Resemblances. 1990. By Edmond Jabès. Translated by Rosmarie Waldrop.

from German

Sonnets to Orpheus. 1987. The poems of Rainer Maria Rilke, translated and with an introduction by David Young.

from Italian

The Coldest Year of Grace: Selected Poems of Giovanni Raboni. 1985. Translated by Stuart Friebert and Vinio Rossi.

from Lithuanian

Chimeras in the Tower: Selected Poems of Henrikas Radauskas. 1986. Translated by Jonas Zdanys.

from Navajo

Hogans: Navajo Houses and House Songs. 1980. Translated by David and Susan McAllester.

from Portuguese

An Anthology of Twentieth-Century Brazilian Poetry. 1972. Edited and with an introduction by Elizabeth Bishop and Emanuel Brasil.

Brazilian Poetry, 1950–1980. 1983. Edited by Emanuel Brasil and William Jay Smith.

When My Brothers Come Home: Poems from Central and Southern Africa. 1985. Edited by Frank Mkalawile Chipasula.

The Alphabet in the Park: Selected Poems of Adélia Prado. 1990. Translated and with an introduction by Ellen Watson.

from Serbian

Roll Call of Mirrors: Selected Poems of Ivan V. Lalić. 1988. Translated by Charles Simic.

from Spanish

Times Alone: Selected Poems of Antonio Machado. 1983. Translated and with an introduction by Robert Bly.

With Walker in Nicaragua and Other Early Poems, 1949–1954. 1984. The poems of Ernesto Cardenal, translated by Jonathan Cohen.

Off the Map: Selected Poems of Gloria Fuertes. 1984. Edited and translated by Philip Levine and Ada Long.

From the Country of Nevermore: Selected Poems of Jorge Teillier. 1990. Translated and with an introduction by Mary Crow.

About the author

Jorge Teillier, who has been called the most important Chilean poet of his generation, was born in Lautaro, in the south of Chile, in 1935. Teillier studied history and geography at the University of Chile, and was later made editor of the University's *Bulletin.* He began writing poems when he was twelve, and his first book of poetry, *Para angeles y gorriones (For Angels and Sparrows)*, was published when he was twenty-one. The author of twelve collections of poems, Teillier has also written many short stories and essays.

Teillier poems focus on the politics of the psyche and are haunted by ill-fated dreams of happiness. Selections from his work have been translated into French, Italian, Rumanian, Russian, Swedish, Polish, and Czechoslovakian. Teillier lives near Santiago, Chile.

About the translator

Mary Crow's interest in Teillier began with a Fulbright research grant to Chile and Peru in 1982. In 1986 Colorado State University, where she is professor of English and director of the Creative Writing Program, awarded her a travel grant to return to Chile to talk with Teillier. She also received an NEA poetry fellowship in 1984 and a second Fulbright to read her poems in Yugoslavia in 1988. She is a graduate of the College of Wooster (B.A.) and of Indiana University (M.A.) and studied at the Writers Workshop at the University of Iowa. She has published three other books of poetry, *Going Home, The Business of Literature,* and *Borders,* and an anthology of poetry by Latin American women poets, which received awards from the NEA and the Columbia University Translation Center. Her home is in Fort Collins, Colorado.

About the book

From the Country of Nevermore was composed on the Mergenthaler 202 in Baskerville, a contemporary rendering of a fine transitional typeface named for the 18th-century English printer John Baskerville. The book was composed by Brevis Press of Bethany, Connecticut, and designed and produced by Kachergis Book Design of Pittsboro, North Carolina.

WESLEYAN POETRY IN TRANSLATION